BEAUT

Beautiful Nowhere

LOUISA CAMPBELL

BOATWHISTLE BOOKS

First published in 2021
by Boatwhistle Books
22 Gloucester Road
Twickenham
London TW2 6NE
United Kingdom

www.boatwhistle.com

Typeset by Boatwhistle in Bell,
with a little American Typewriter on the side

A catalogue record for this book
is available from the British Library

ISBN 978-1-911052-04-3

Printed in the United Kingdom by TJ Books, Padstow,
on 80 gsm Munken Premium paper

Contents

[III]

[IV]

[**I**]

And what did you want?
To call myself beloved, to feel myself
beloved on the earth.
—RAYMOND CARVER, 'Late Fragment'

Dawning

Sometimes, when the party's heave
is bigger than the people there,
love slips softly past the buffet,
between the clinking glasses
and out of the back door.

Love kicks off her high heels, hurries
barefoot in her red silk dress
into the night.
She lifts her right hand,
grips the sky's edge tight,
and as she leaves, she pulls it
down behind her.

The sky falls, magnificent
as a tumbling ballroom chandelier.

And in the daylight
we're left gaping.
What's this, lying flat,
lifeless round our feet?
What is it?

Triggers

Especially, bubbles
in a little girl's hands

the colour green, a kind of dusty sage green

purple, like the purple in the velvet in the crown
on that day trip to the Tower of London,
and that can't be my favourite colour
any more

London

Brighton
small hotels
strawberry ice cream
seagulls
buckets
spades

the smell of stale urine
the smell of stale urine in alleys
alleys

straw hats
straw hats on uncles
uncles
men.

Ballum Rancum

I don't think—
how they sailed me down
to the cellar of the Earth,
left behind lover, baby,
for a lace collar,
loaf of bread.

I don't look—
my nakedness,
grinning eyes,
the numbers they painted
on our backs
in black;
the five is a viper,
the nought is a noose.

I don't listen—
the clapping,
the offer to buy me
for a barrel of rum,
endless thudding
of bare feet on wood.

I just feel the little flame inside me
flicker.

Nests

I remember the joy of outside,
where I couldn't hear Mum and Dad
in the kitchen, the front door slam,
especially if I sang . . .

The birds up in the treetops sing their song
They sing their joyful music all day long

Called in for tea, I found a thrush on the path,
its head and body soft cold lumps,
its feet twisted twigs. I turned it over,
saw tiny black bugs in its split-open belly.

I found a Cook's Matches box,
tucked it in with sheets of pink Andrex,
dripped Calpol into its open beak,
waited for it to get better.

Application Form

If I write that I deserve this
—that I'm worthwhile, good,
accomplished—
then my mother will be wrong

and I want her to be right;
I want to be *problematic*
with my *skewed view,*
my *vivid imagination.*

I want to sob, *Mum,*
you were right all along,
let her fold me in, her soft cardigan
buttoned behind my back.

The cardigan is sunshine yellow,
the buttons white plastic daisies.

Or was that *my* cardigan,
my daisy buttons?

Boy

Often, Boy is tied and beaten by Mum & Dad. Boy learns to tiptoe around the house. Boy locks Tied & Beaten in the cupboard where they shout and rattle the doorknob.

Boy calls Teacher *wanker*, but Teacher does not tie or beat him. This feels like love. Sometimes Boy plays truant in Albert Park, but still Teacher does not beat him. This also feels like love.

In Albert Park, Boy meets Strongbow. Boy likes Strongbow's name, the taste of him. Drinking Strongbow feels like the opposite of screaming, and the more Boy drinks, the quieter Tied & Beaten become in the cupboard. Strongbow feels like Love.

Strongbow costs four jobs, a wife and a child, but Tied & Beaten are still in the cupboard, and Boy has become the best tiptoer in the county.

Boy tiptoes through his friend Billy's Barclays bank account, through his cousin Debbie's pink leather purse. He tiptoes in and out of the big detached houses in Cavendish Drive. He tiptoes through the oak-panelled courtroom, past the judge's horsehair wig.

Boy tiptoes back to his attic flat, above Karl's Kebabs on the London Road. The flat is empty apart from a brown sleeping bag and a white mug. Tied & Beaten are in the cupboard and Boy sits on the floor with Strongbow. *I love my life*, says Boy.

The Red Box

I keep thinking of the antique china doll
she handed down to me when I was ten.
Look, she said, *when I was your age*
I gave her your name! And there,
embroidered on its plain blue cotton dress:
my name in yellow thread.
I emptied out my big red sewing box
to put my fragile doll in, keep it safe.

When I had children of my own,
she brought that box to my house, left it,
like a foundling, outside my front door.
It felt as if there was a stone
inside my throat as I opened the lid.
But nestling in the padded satin red
was nothing.

Forever

At night, in your frilled white gown
you hold your candelabra high.

Pipes clank-rattle,
tarnished taps gush blood.
Flies buzz, or, upside-down,
crust windowsills.

From the attic, a silent scream,
rumble of empty rocking chair
on worn wood boards.
Downstairs, faintly, a piano.

When the morning sun sings
through stone window frames
—even after toast,
fresh tea and kedgeree—

you shudder at shrieks
from your cellar.
Some things remain there,
tethered.

She

was waiting for me
before I was born.

Sometimes she clearly says
my name,
leaves it hanging.

More often, whispers so softly
I can't hear, but only see
the words behind my eyes.

She's an ember just behind my left shoulder;
wisp on the nape of my neck; shove
that wobbles me like a rickety table;
tug from a child wanting its mother.

She couldn't wait to spell out her name,
whizz the glass across the board,
tell me I'm a *F-O-O-L*.

She followed me home,
flashed her face in the bathroom mirror;
so dark, those eyes,
no windows in the room.

I tried to lose her with potions,
beads, incantations.
Thought I'd won until
she set my wind chimes tinkling.

I tried to escape to churches,
sat at the back with hassocks,
fusty prayer books,
but I could only stand that so long.

Then I wrote her into a story,
bricked her up, thought,
That'll teach her!

But the absence cut deep,
so I wrote instead
that she escaped,
departed on a train.

One day she might
come back again.

Deliver Us

They're coming.

> *We don't know whether we're nervous.*

We're nervous.

> *Not nervous.*

What to wear?

> *We wear jeans.*
> *We took off the white top*
> *and put on the green one.*

It's maybe OK,
these things matter.

> *They don't matter*

> *and they're knocking on our door*
> *now.*

We let them in,

> *we smile,*

but think
we shouldn't be smiling.
We stop.

> *Then start again.*
> *Pastor Dave is wearing that polo shirt*
> *with blue and brown stripes.*
> *Blue looks crap with brown.*

Do we really think that,
or is it in our head from a *Cosmopolitan*
we read years ago?

Jean's here;
the most boring person in the world.

That's cruel—she's here for our sake.
She's brought a bucket.

A bright orange bucket.

Dave starts with the prayers
like he would at the meeting:
'Please, Lord, bless our sister,

deliver from evil, blah blah . . .'

We're disappointed it's not
'Exorcizamus te, omnis immundus spiritus',

but it's the twenty-first century,
for God's sake.

Dave says we should say the Lord's Prayer
and we do.

I do

and that's when this pull starts
from way down inside me,

like peeling thick, rubbery clingfilm
up through my guts
and out of the top of my head.
I think I'll puke,
but I don't,
I spit.
I spit into Jean's orange bucket.

Dave says 'Praise Jesus!'
Jean says 'Hallelujah!'
I say 'Amen',
but feel raw,
thin,
empty.

I want them to go.
I hold out the bucket.
Jean takes it

and they've gone.
I go to my room,
curl up on the bed.
The world's

stopped.

It's quiet.
I'm the only soul here.

I start shaking,
big sobs blubbing
out of my mouth
like toads,
and through toads
I find myself calling her,
calling her back

and the next thing we know,

we're smiling.

Feral You

Oh no, no, no, do not forgive!
Grab on tight to all your grief.
Don't take your fury by the arm
and frogmarch it into the street:
it will survive on scraps of thoughts
and memories left out for it

and sometimes scrawny, sometimes sleek,
at night-time it will stand and screech
as bold as brawn, outside your gate,
when you're grown up,
when it's too late.

[**II**]

How can we put our woundedness in the service of others?
—HENRI J. M. NOUWEN, *The Wounded Healer*

The Ward

It's not the jump-proof windows,
     collapsible, noose-defying hinges,
nor the glint of the hook-shaped ligature-cutter
     in matron's locked cupboard.
It's not the shake of the ward clerk's small hand
     as she picks up the phone,
the doctor's careful avoidance of eye contact,
     nurses' cheery smiles.
It's not the little lock of grey hair
     in the corner of the non-slip floor,
nor the amber stains
     on the wipe-clean duvet.
It's not the scent of Dettol mingling with
     lunch-time's fried fish,
rattle of the drug trolley, thud
     of the filing cabinet drawer.
It's not even the chain on the hospital teaspoon
     in the patients' wary kitchen.
It's the long white corridor that carries you

     from

        nothing

       to

   nowhere.

Room 3

It was just before dawn when she
stopped.
Middle lane of the M25.
Unclunked her seatbelt, opened the door,
got out, walked barefoot
to the front of her Ford
and stood.
Gazing ahead, not seeing
lorries swerve past; not feeling
the backdrafts ruffle her hair;
not hearing horns blasting.

A van driver brought her in:
she was lucky.
We must find her some slippers.
She works in a shop. No kids.
There's an uncle somewhere;
we'll try to locate him.

Still, in her hospital nightie,
stuck in that spot
at the foot of her bed,
staring . . .

Say? She says only one phrase
(makes you jump when she speaks):

I have seen myself.

Yes, that's it—nothing more—
then goes on staring.

When we write together

you can write the dusty creeper
tangled round the chestnut tree.
You can write the shears to cut,
or strength to pull the creeper off.

If you can't write the strength or cut,
then you can write the flames that grow,
the bonfire that we build; or you can
wait and write the embers.

If you can't write the embers,
you can write the rain that puts them out,
or you can write the breeze that shifts the clouds;
the sun that waits behind them.

If you can't write the sun,
then write the bird that comes to sit up in the tree.
If you can't write the bird, then write its song,
because it's your song, and you'll know it.

Glowing Report

The whispering tinfoil shroud silvers
your fridge, cooker, washing machine.
Your tablets laid out—one, two, three—
not taken. We will not speak of them.

The sun will beam through your window,
turn the foil to a tide of gold.
We'll bathe in the lighting up of it
and the smile from our eyes will tether us.

When you are better, when I leave,
asking *Was it the meds or the CBT that worked?*,
you'll say it was our glow from the foil
as the voices chittered behind it.

Paperwork

In dribs and drabs
the patients come to the office door.
Not now, say the nurses, *we're writing
    the notes.*

In twos and threes
the patients come to the office door.
Not now, say the nurses, *we're filling in
    risk assessments.*

At sixes and sevens
the patients come to the office door.
Not now, say the nurses, *we're completing
    an incident form to report we've run out
    of incident forms.*

Now all the patients come out of their rooms.
Sideways, they line the corridor,
join hands and feet,
turn into paper.

They concertina through the front door
and into the car park.
Before the nurses can grab them,
they rustle, flap,

take off,

float up,

away on the breeze.

Nightline

To me, he is in a silent movie,
white face, black-eyelined eyes,
holding up a sign,
'I can't go on!'

I picture him
at the top of a towering tenement,
bass piano trembling,
honky-tonk,
ready to leap—

saved by two men in overalls
who carry a bulging mattress
along the grey pavement below.

I picture a steam train
coming closer, closer—
sputtering to a stop
before he can jump.

In my office, blue carpet, red phone,
I barter my rainbow ideas
for his black ones and white ones.

He has to agree that life in Technicolor
holds more hope than
silence,
black and white signs,
and anyway, a whole house could collapse
and leave him simply brushing the plaster dust
from his shoulders.

Just before I click the phone down,
I hear white pills rattle
from a grey bottle.

I smile and dial
for a bright yellow ambulance.

Flags

The care plan was sorted:
emergency numbers; children in foster;
no bleach in the house; her blue tablets.

An old hand, I'd learned
as I closed every front door behind me
to slam shut a heavier door in my mind.

So often she'd told me the story
of Grandad, the day at Skegness,
the donkey ride bribe for keeping their secret.

But this time, she mentioned the swimsuit:
bikini with triangle top and trunk bottoms,
all patterned in Union Jacks.

As I walked to the car clutching diary and briefcase,
my mind filled with crosses and kisses,
shrieking and dancing in red, white and blue.

Art Therapy

She chooses pastels, sugar paper,
draws a face with *rose pink* cheeks,
eyes with *cornflower blue*,
sunshine yellow hair, in bunches.

She bites her lip,
draws gingham bows
in *springtime green*
to tie the bunches up.

A mouth that, like hers,
neither smiles nor frowns,
carnation pink.
She colours in the spaces, *flesh*.

She takes a liquid glue tube,
stretches arms up big and tall,
upends the tube, and squeezes.
Milk-white globules splat down

on her pastel face.
Her hands keep squeezing
till the tube is empty.

The Sticky

It's shit-brown, snot-grey, tar-black,
spewing over the rim of their sack
as they hug it to their chest,
push open the door with their back,
shuffle across to the chair.

They sit, clutching it on their lap,
peeping over the top.
They can't put it down, not
yet, not yet.

They talk of that and this.
Sometimes they mention the sticky;
reach round the sack for the tissues.

Sometimes they empty it
into the air between us;
the sticky drops to the floor
in globules and puddles;
the sack exhales.
They leave the room, lighter.

But I have to clear up when they've gone
and the stench of the sticky clings;
the taste squats hefty on my stomach.
I vomit it up,
or at night, spit it out in my dreams.

Concrete

That twelve-hour shift, she walked 3.6 miles
on the white non-slip floor, in low-heeled
black leather lace-up shoes.

When it was time for medication, she flustered
over milligrams and millimoles.

She wrote notes for forty patients and two incident
forms (in triplicate) with a black Bic biro.

At teatime, in the office, she ate a sausage roll
she had bought on the way to work
from the One Stop.

She looked up
at the moon
above the roof
of the Arndale Centre
on her way home, and thought
it looked like concrete.

At bedtime, she lay flat on her back
on her small bed
and turned off her bedside lamp.

Moon

That twelve-hour shift, he tugged his feet as if
through treacle from his single room to the canteen
and back three times. He wore blue flip-flops.

When it was time for medication, he considered
side effects.

He wrote *FUCK OFF* on his bedroom wall with the
charcoal from four burnt matches.

At teatime, in the canteen, he ate macaroni cheese,
surrounded by thirty-nine other patients,
also eating macaroni cheese.

He looked up at the moon sitting just above the
hospital incinerator chimney and couldn't remember
whether it ever met up with the sun. He thought one
day he would walk to the Planetarium in London
because they would know, and because you can walk
around London and no one notices you.

At bedtime, he lay flat on his back
on his plastic-covered hospital mattress
and the ward strip lights blinked off.

Sandbags

You have welly boots,
blue as balloons,
so you can wobble the streetlights' glow
as you splunch in puddles.

You have a mac,
banana yellow,
so you can spin with your arms outstretched
in the drizzle and chill.

I will buckle my shoe
and push through grey;
push the buggy, grip the handles,
shopping hanging sandbag-heavy.

Tonight,
in blackness,
I'll hold a torch for you
to flame away the dark.

Bulky Waste Collection

The bin men groan beneath the weight.
I feel so girly, handing up cushions.
By the truck, I had expected crumbs,
pen tops, maybe even 10p,
but not the old cellophane wrapper
from his Lambert & Butler.

The kindest thing he did for me
was to go outside to smoke.
Now I picture my tatty sofa, teetering
on the tip of a slagheap-sized mountain
of rubbish. And him, seated on it,
king of all he surveys,
lighting up.

The Drop

A schoolboy
stands
alone
in the church
and sings.
The robin
on the fence
by the ash path
flits away.
The grass
on the verges
outside the flats
turns black.
The sun
is tarnished.
Iron
clangs
shut
around you.
You start to
fall.
There is nothing
you can do.
Your television
spouts evil.

Your bread
is poisoned.
Your living room curtains
have turned to fire,
the flames are grey.
You have been longing
for the rain,
but now it falls
and falls
as acid.
The moon
has been stolen.
Everything
is darkness
and you,
especially,
are darkness.
Outside each
front door,
a thorn.
Protruding
from every chimney pot,
a riddle.
Everyone lies,
beetles

crawling
from their mouths.
You are
still falling.
The schoolboy
stops
singing.

[**III**]

You have to keep breaking your heart until it opens.

—RUMI

(No Hood)

pack all toiletries
shower flip-flops are essential

paper, envelopes, pens (no springs)
stamps will be OK

dressing gown (no hood)
it is best not to tell

wear a cheap watch
you should be allowed to keep it on

don't let them see
do not delay

lots of underwear (no Y-fronts)
a fleece (no hood)

tinned meat such as Spam or corned beef
tinned custard

when you least expect
locked away

here to help
such a massive threat

the right thing
your sticky label

no laces, no belt
the priest (no hood)

if you try to leave
you can't

I Was Not Psychotic
in that Coffee Shop
in Blackburn

Big cloud cakes squidge-giggled
beneath glass dome sparkles;
the old wooden pew squeaked its welcome.
A man read a crisp, new *Guardian*.

Behind him, the warmth of pitched pine panels,
above him, floral wallpaper stems
danced like chorus girls' legs.
My favourite place; my cheery-up place.

It was, until

the moment the coffee machine shrieked
its steam-pressured whistle,
at just that moment, the man
with the newspaper folded it,
picked up his coffee cup,
stared straight at me;

instead of eyes,
there was a fire.

Shh . . .

. . . you won't see him,

solitary,
sidling up at the bus stop,
faceless in the shadows,
stealing snippets.

You won't notice him
scribbling silently
beneath a black umbrella
in the slanting rain.

Later—years later—
you'll turn a page
and a line, or a phrase, will
twinkle,
startle you
with its truth.

You'll never know
that thought was yours
all along.

All at Sea

His mood floats silently, steel in dark water:
a sea mine, ancient, but ready to blow.

Baccy-stained fingers grip empty green cup
while he steadily sways, as if with the waves.

Sometimes, in the depths of the navy-blue night,
he flounders; his limbs start to twitch and tread
    water.

His memories; tendrils, cut off, but still wriggling.
Thoughts clang like a warning bell far from the
    shore.

One day his voice will come in with the tide,
writhing with squid from the clutter of ocean

or rising in inky-dark bubbles with kraken:
I want to come up now, bloop-bloop, bloop-bloop.

Real Dereal

These are not the walls I painted.
This is not the blue sofa I bought.

No, I won't sit down.
I can feel this room stare
at the back of my neck.

It's true my heavy feet brought me,
as if they knew the way,
and it's true the Yale in my pocket
fits the lock in the grey front door.

But I've never been here before;
I can't stay.

If only I'd tied a red thread,
unspooled, held tight
to find my way home.

But where to attach it?
There was nowhere.

Coconut Shells

I.

I promised myself I would not look through the
    closed window at the church tower clock again.
From this silent room I can see its blue tarnished face,
black iron hands and numerals.
I cannot hear the chunk and whirr of cogs and
    spindles.

When I hear twelve low, heavy chimes
I will attach my veil to my silver headdress.

High overhead, a sickly light gropes through these
    clouds.

Now I hear horses' hooves.
As a child, I made the sound with coconut shells.
Mother says, even though I'm too good for him,
    I must have a carriage.

I promised myself I would not look through the
    closed window at the church tower clock again,
so I find myself counting.
Mother says it takes exactly one second to say the
    word 'elephant'.

II.

She promised herself she would not look up at the
    white plastic asylum canteen clock
again.
She sits, in white wedding dress, at a yellow table;
    the others are vacant,
apart from the one where the nurse sits, silently,
    watching.

The kitchen staff have gone home.
The cleaner starts to sweep the white floor with a
    soft brush.
What's left of the evening sun glints on the bride's
    tiara, then sinks away.

The taffeta skirt engulfs the chair, fills the space
    beneath the table.
Her veil tangles around a chair leg.
She has her bouquet: yellow and ivory roses, yellow
    chrysanthemums,
daisies, shaped into a heart.
She picks the petals out one by one. They fall on the
    yellow table
and the white floor.

She promised herself she would not look up at the
    white plastic hospital canteen clock
again
so she whispers, 'elephant, elephant . . .'

The cleaner's broom swishes.

Changeling

(MENTAL HEALTH NURSE, SECTIONED)

I.

Not through the staff door with my M&S prawn
sandwich, but collected from reception, shunted to a
side room, told to sit and wait.

I didn't work on wards, I worked in the community,
but they know who I am. The nurse admitting does
his breezy best to smile, then stares at his grey folder,
so I can almost see the short straw poking out from
his shirt pocket. He tries to tell me how I must be
feeling. I don't feel like that at all.

II.

When I was training, a student asked the tutor, *Do
mental health nurses go mad, too?* The lecture hall held
its breath.

III.

Alone in the craft room (grey Formica tables, pad-locked cupboards), I check if I can jump out of the windows, but they're iron-framed and bolted shut.

John, a patient, comes to introduce himself and tell me I should come and meet them all; they're friendly, and joining in will help me get well soon. He introduces me to Tom and Stella. Aisha's here, I used to do her jab at depot clinic. She smiles, *You always said 'One— two—three—breathe, so it won't hurt'*.

IV.

Water splats from the bath tap. There's no plug, so we can't drown ourselves. Stella told me to fetch paper hand towels from the toilets and pack them tightly in the plughole. Someone knocks, *Unlock this door, we need to see you!* It dawns on me that I must be on obs. Apart from when admitting, that's the only time a nurse speaks to me.

V.

I dreamed I was thirsty. I turned on the tap, but the water gushed out black.

VI.

I don't understand the duvet covers in the dormitory. One side's a sort of rubbery material with yellow stains. I beg for sleep, glancing at the clock at 2.15, 3.20, 4.30. One of the three night staff bellows through the door for us to get our heads down. Then they slurp Red Bull from cans they scrunch up when empty, drop on the corridor floor and leave to rattle underneath their seats.

VII.

We talk together on vinyl easy chairs in the patients' lounge.

Aisha brings me buttered toast and cups of kindness from the hall machine.

Tom touches my arm, tells me he's been like a kitten, trying to unravel wool. *It's better to just let things be,* he says.

When John walks with me in the garden, he shows me lime green crocus tips, clambering up through dusty leaves and brick-hard mud.

Not There

When people ask about my dad,
I'm ransacking my memory's
narrow aisles of shelves of files,
to find my father's breakdown.
My feet thup-thup on rolling ladders
trundle-shuddering forward, back.
I shake the folders upside-down—
a sparsely scribbled sheet of A4 flutters out.

Today I met my son in Caffè Nero,
asked him, in between *Americano?*
and *How's work?*, what he can remember
from that dark time when I
broke. I feel him close a folder,
shove it firmly back up on the shelf.
You know . . . he says, *sorry Mum,*
I try hard not to think of that.

But I've never put away
the big black box file
with a hunched boy googling,
15, mother sectioned,
will I be taken into care?

Look, this file is big enough
for me to climb inside
and close the lid.

My Family Is Our DNA's Own Personal Theme Park

Little sprite gene, little imp, rogue,
        helter-skelters through my family's

        DNA, guffaws, twists
the cloth we're cut from, meddles,

  cackles as a Morris Minor pulls up
at the madhouse,

      Grandma Pat shouts in her
        powder pink raffia hat, gets out.

      Our gene tee-hees as Dad, with his
  overnight bag, trembles his way

across the yard to the ward.
    Rascal gene, rapscallion, hear our scallywag

        chortle at both my bankruptcies,
    each crass divorce.

  Nobody knows, but I watch my daughter, her gait,
  her eyes; analyse her teenage pronouncements

for logic, notice if she wakes too early,
sleeps for too long. This morning,

she says she thought she saw
a shadow watch her sleep

from the end of her bed.
We laugh.

But as she slams her bedroom door
behind her,

something squeaks like a rusty hinge,
like a floorboard,

like a mouse,
like a mischievous little snigger.

Amniocentesis

In slow motion, you turned
as the needle intruded
on your liquid world,
flipped to your front,
lifted your head to see—
nose to needle.

My darling, my little one,
if only you'd sampled my essence
to test if I would be normal
enough, healthy enough
to be your mother;

I'd have turned to face you,
banged the inside of the screen,
swiped my finger across my throat,
tried to make you hear me shouting,
No! No! No!

Finding Nico

Was it her, dancing on top of a hundred-foot pole,
calling the world to come up?

Was it her high that married the stranger?
Was it her low that divorced him?

Each year she signs up to save the world; each year
    she drops
out, feeling the air pressing down like an anvil.

She cries. She laughs. She says,
My life is a party that nobody comes to.

Often, she feels like screaming;
sometimes she does—

it sounds like a fountain of glass.
She sees herself in the pieces,

the same way lost treasures are found
while searching for something else.

[IV]

. . . there was a new voice
which you slowly
recognised as your own . . .

—MARY OLIVER, 'The Journey'

Seafront, January

No need to talk. If we spoke,
our words would be drowned
by the thunderous waves,
carried away on the easterly wind
that sticks our hair to our faces,
flips sun-bleached bunting
at kiosks' closed shutters.

Look how the smooth wide wave
moves steadily, rolling, surging
to shore, where it fizzes to foam,
flattens and lets itself fall
back, as if arriving is no more
than leaving again.

Look at the edgeless horizon:
a nothingness, simply
the furthest we can see;
a beautiful nowhere.

We disappear here, as if the sea
absorbs our watery bodies;
our thoughts pulled in, then out
by the tide, the silvery sun.

Riggwelter

I've stopped thinking about the falling;
how it happened before I understood
the sound like a hill imploding
was me, hitting grass.

I've given up
on the struggle-jolting;
past caring about the frowns
of the upright, staring, chewing.

Grateful for my fleece
in clammy dew,
with this new upside-down life
I see beyond my waggling hooves

to the sky.
Today the wind scuffles
through the grass at my ears.
Tonight there will be stars.

Carried

I love him because he's perfected the art
of flinging his towel through the shower room window
to land on the airer below.

I love him because he can't dance,
but he sings like a minstrel
and nobody knows.

I love him because he can size people up in an instant
and save me the trouble
of being dismayed.

I love him because, even though his hair's grey now,
to me he's the boy scoring tries for the school
and mucking about in the end-of-term play.

I love him because we're both rootless from moving
so often, it feels we're incessantly blown
like leaves, over hills, over cities and oceans,

learning the wind is our strength
and together is home.

Beads

For Kate

The things she said
and what she didn't
pulled me two hundred miles to meet her—
kindness between the lines,
shared tears, understanding.

We said we'd meet in the hotel lobby:
vast; wall-to-wall glass;
swishing steel lift doors;
reception desk, indifferent.
I stood small at the window
and waited.

She arrived, in glamour and timidity,
I'm so pleased to meet you . . . she said
to the floor
but sorry, I'm socially awkward.

She fiddled with beads in her bracelet.
Silent, side by side,
we looked out.

Grey city streets,
cars, buses and people
went who-knows-where,
who-knows-why.

Pulteney Weir

I want it like this, but
without the dark water,
without the signs: *NO DIVING!*
KEEP OUT!

I want to rest here, but
without the water's rush and hiss,
the single-leafed twig transfixed
between two currents.

Walking the dear familiar streets,
memories ghoul like children
who run ahead and hide
behind bins and lamp posts

to jump out at their mothers.
I want to come home.
I want to come down to the weir
and sit, like I used to.

But this water,
this dread-green water;
it dampens my face
and I'm not even crying.

Harrison's Rocks

Leafless branches beckon and you wince,
but find the bitterness has gone;
a warm breeze strokes your face.
The rocks that glowered charcoal-grey
are honey-coloured now.

You don't need courage any more.
You trample clingy brambles with your lighter feet,
find you no longer struggle,
but leap over a tumbled trunk

and see it, not as an obstacle,
but an exhibit of soft moss.
You notice tender violets
you've forgotten, or not seen before.
Next time this way will be easier still.

Today the amiable rocks
are topped with a surprising blue
and have new ridges, which might work as steps.
An unseen smile is traced upon your face.

You think you'll have a go
at climbing up.

Work Capability Assessment

They may as well strap you to a wooden chair,
slap you about a bit,
dim lightbulb over your head.

Tell us exactly how far you can walk
before you must stop
for the pain ...

Did you know
there's a wheelchair
imagined for you?

If they imagine you
having the strength to propel it,
you fail.

Census

With the creak in the board she used to hear,
I push up the sash she used to open.

She presses her raw hands to the window sill,
looks across to the red terrace,
bricks wobbling through this flaw in the glass.

With her back to her eight children's beds,
she breathes autumn air,
looks above and beyond to the hills.

I place my hands on hers, feel
her widow's strength.

She senses me, two centuries ahead,
turns hands palm-up to hold mine, whispers,

Short, precious it is;
you barely feel the kiss of its wings,
then you must let it go.

Not Pastel People

Last night, we'd not kept a bag packed
at the back of the wardrobe;

not hidden in cupboards, listening,
wide-eyed, not listening;

considered the bed size for cardboard;
searched helplines; hovered

outside the police station door,
walked on, walked back.

I wake thinking life will be pink sugar mice,
primrose soft velvet and candy floss blue;

air will slip warm
with the gentlest of breeze, but

if you lobbed a ball at me now
it would not bounce, only
thud. Tepid. Dead.

The air is.
I am.

I look to the shape of my scars—
the sting of the red revives me.

I stand with my rickety spine
and yell like the gold

in the cracks of a kintsugi vase,
I'm alive! alive! alive!

Does it Jiggle?

'Does it still jiggle?'
'Yes! It jiggles.'
'Does it still quiver?'
'Yes, it does.'
'Does it still sparkle?'
'Yes! It sparkles and shimmers and glows!'
'Does it still smell of hope?'
'Oh, I'm not sure if it still smells of hope . . .'
'Of hope and joy?'
'Maybe of joy, but I'm not sure about hope.'

'Does it still sing, then?'
'Sing?'
'Sing! Does it still sing?'
'Did it ever sing?'
'Yes! It sang with a tune that could lift stompy
    boots up out of mud; put red and yellow
    biplanes in blue.'
'I don't think it ever sang,'
'Yes, it sang, and each note was a bird on a branch,
    and the tree was the Earth and the Earth was
    the sun and it warmed us through to our bones,
    so we'd take off our jumpers and tie them round
    our waists by the arms, and walk with our
    heads up and our shoulders down.'

'Maybe I remember the melody; maybe I do . . .'
'Like birds and biplanes and warmth?'
'I do, I do remember!'
'So the hope? You can smell the hope now?'
'Yes, I can smell it!'

Thank goodness,
thank goodness it still jiggles,
and quivers, and sparkles, and shimmers and glows!

Notes

'Ballum Rancum' (page 6)   Women transported to
Norfolk Island as prisoners were sold as slaves. Every
Thursday night in the soldiers' barracks, they danced a
naked 'ballum rancum', with numbers painted on their
backs to identify them to prospective purchasers.

'Changeling' (page 54)   'Obs' is short for nurses' regular
observations of patients considered at risk, such as
constant obs for high risk and maybe fifteen-minute
intervals, then half-hourly, and so on as the risk
diminishes. 'Depot' is a long-lasting intramuscular
injection, in this case, of antipsychotic medication,
usually given monthly at a clinic. It's considered
preferable for patients who may forget to take tablets
daily, and become unwell.

'Riggwelter' (page 68)   Although the poem describes a
whimsically pleasant picture of riggwelter, should you
come across a sheep on its back with its legs in the air,
it would be at risk of dying from suffocation, and you
should immediately find a farmer to come and rescue it.

Acknowledgements

Some of these poems, or versions of them, have previously appeared in the pamphlets *The Happy Bus* (Picaroon Poetry) and *The Ward* (Paper Swans Press). Others have appeared in the following journals: *Atrium, Clear Poetry, The Interpreter's House, Lapidus Journal, Lonesome October Lit, The North, Obsessed With Pipework, One Hand Clapping, The Open Mouse, Picaroon, Prole, Riggwelter, The Royal Society of Psychiatrists (South Eastern) Newsletter* and *Stand.*

'Work Capability Assessment' was published in *The Brown Envelope Book* (Caparison/Culture Matters in collaboration with Don't Go Breaking Our Arts). 'Not Pastel People' appeared in *Flapdoodle,* a handmade pamphlet by the artist kazvina, who also provided the cover art for this book.

Thanks are due to the poets and teachers whose advice and wisdom has helped create these poems: Carrie Etter, Anne-Marie Fyfe, Ira Lightman, Jess Mookherjee, Clare Shaw, the Sussex Sticks Poetry Group, Julia Webb, Jackie Wills, and to John McCullough, who started it all.

Also to the incredible, supportive poetry community (names too numerous to mention, but you know who you are), and to my rock, Helen Mcloughlin.

Finally, to Hamish Ironside, who can take a half and make a beautiful whole.